Follow The
FOOD
CHAIN

Who Ate the Penguin?

AN OCEAN FOOD CHAIN

Sarah Ridley

Crabtree Publishing Company
www.crabtreebooks.com

CRABTREE
PUBLISHING COMPANY
WWW.CRABTREEBOOKS.COM

Author: Sarah Ridley

Editorial director: Kathy Middleton

Editors: Nicola Edwards, Ellen Rodger

Proofreader: Crystal Sikkens

Designer: Lisa Peacock

Prepress technician: Samara Parent

Print coordinator: Katherine Berti

Photo credits:
Alamy: Colin Harris/era-images 7.
FLPA Images/Minden Pictures: Flip Nicklin 9; Norbert Wu 10c.
iStock: jrphoto6 14c; mlharing 5.
Nature PL: Ben Cranke 16c; Kaslowski 11t.
Shutterstock: Big Foot Productions 20-21bg; Simon Brockington 17c; Rich Carey front cover t, 10br, 12br, 14br, 16br, 18br, 21cl; ChameleonsEye 12c, 13bl, 15bl, 17bl, 19bl, 21bl; Igor Chaykovsky 23t; diverdog 4; Robert McGillivray 1, 19c; polarman 33b; Alexey Seafarer front cover cr; Nattawit Sronrachrudee 6bl, 8bl, 10bl, 12bl, 14bl, 16bl, 18bl, 20cl; stephenallen75 11c; james_stone76 13c; Tarpan front cover cl & b, 8c, 8br, 10bcr, 12bcr, 14bcr, 16bcr, 17bcl, 18c, 18bcr, 19bcl, 20cr, 21br; Fredy Thuerig 15tl; TravelMediaProductions 22; Robert Tripodi 19bcr, 21tr; vladsilver 2, 15cr.
Wikimedia Commons: Professor Gordon Taylor, Stony Brook University PD 6c & bc, 8bc, 10bc,12bcl, 14bcl, 16bcl, 18bcl, 20b.

Every attempt has been made to clear copyright. Should there be any inadvertent omission please apply to the publisher for rectification.

Library and Archives Canada Cataloguing in Publication

Title: Who ate the penguin? : an ocean food chain / Sarah Ridley.
Names: Ridley, Sarah, 1963- author.
Description: Series statement: Follow the food chain |
  Previously published: London: Wayland, 2019. | Includes index.
Identifiers: Canadiana (print) 20190194987 |
  Canadiana (ebook) 20190194995 |
  ISBN 9780778771425 (hardcover) |
  ISBN 9780778771463 (softcover) |
  ISBN 9781427124531 (HTML)
Subjects: LCSH: Marine ecology—Juvenile literature. |
  LCSH: Food chains (Ecology)—Antarctica—Juvenile literature.
Classification: LCC QH84.2 .R53 2020 | DDC j508.989—dc23

Library of Congress Cataloging-in-Publication Data

Names: Ridley, Sarah, 1963- author.
Title: Who ate the penguin? : an ocean food chain / Sarah Ridley.
Description: New York : Crabtree Publishing Company, 2020. |
  Series: Follow the food chain | Includes index.
Identifiers: LCCN 2019043666 (print) | LCCN 2019043667 (ebook) |
  ISBN 9780778771425 (hardcover) |
  ISBN 9780778771463 (paperback) |
  ISBN 9781427124531 (ebook)
Subjects: LCSH: Food chains (Ecology)--Juvenile literature. |
  Marine ecology--Juvenile literature.
Classification: LCC QH541.15.F66 R537 2020 (print) | LCC QH541.15.
  F66 (ebook) | DDC 577/.16--dc23
LC record available at https://lccn.loc.gov/2019043666
LC ebook record available at https://lccn.loc.gov/2019043667

Crabtree Publishing Company

www.crabtreebooks.com   1–800–387–7650
Published by Crabtree Publishing Company in 2020

First published in Great Britain in 2019 by Wayland
Copyright ©Hodder and Stoughton, 2019

Printed in the U.S.A./012020/CG20191115

Published in Canada
Crabtree Publishing
616 Welland Ave.
St. Catharines, Ontario
L2M 5V6

Published in the United States
Crabtree Publishing
PMB 59051
350 Fifth Avenue, 59th Floor
New York, New York 10118

CONTENTS

Food for living

All living things need food to give them the **energy** to live. Plants make their own food using energy from sunlight, air, soil, and water.

In seas and oceans, seaweed uses sunlight to help make its own food.

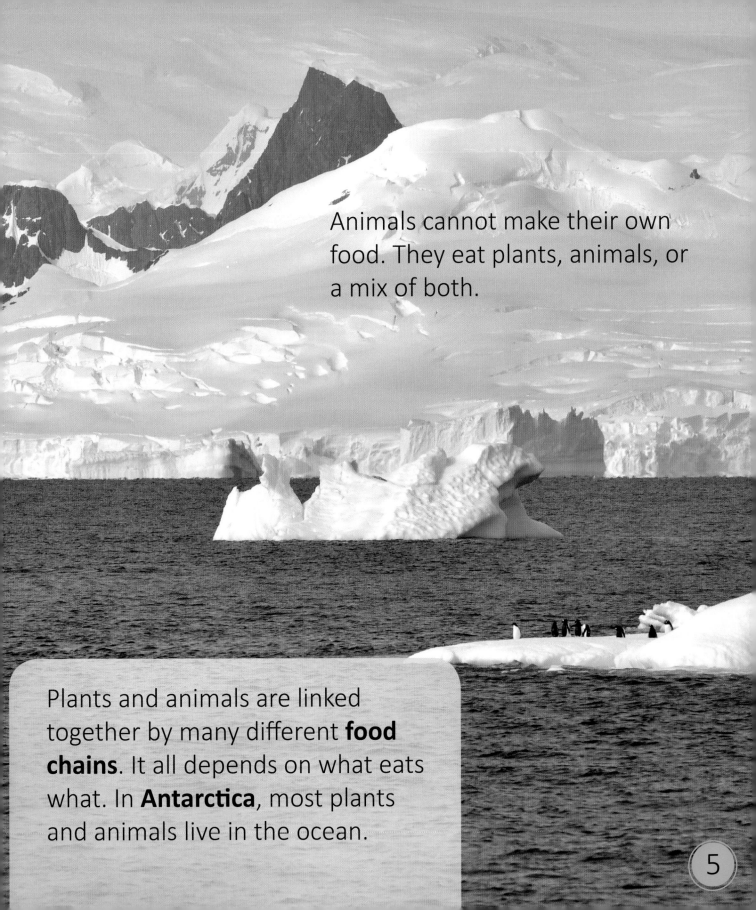

Animals cannot make their own food. They eat plants, animals, or a mix of both.

Plants and animals are linked together by many different **food chains**. It all depends on what eats what. In **Antarctica**, most plants and animals live in the ocean.

The start of the food chain

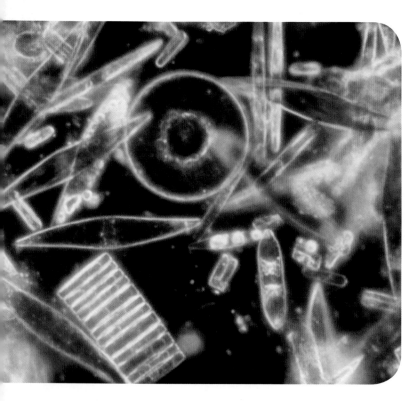

Plant plankton are at the start, or bottom, of every ocean food chain. Millions of these tiny water plants float in the ocean. They are too small for us to see unless we use a **microscope**.

← Antarctic plankton

↓ In a food chain, an arrow shows the food energy moving from one living thing to another.

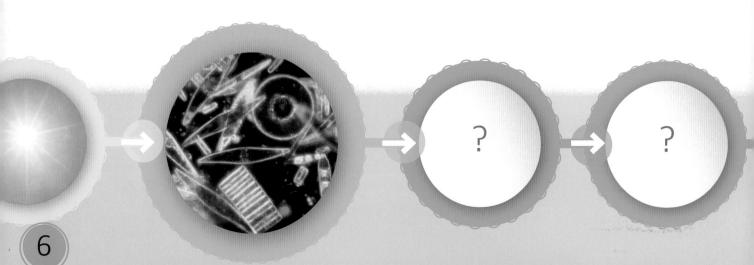

? ?

There are many different kinds of plant plankton. They all use energy from sunlight and **nutrients** in the ocean to make their own food.

Some plankton float on top of the ocean. Others grow under the ice. The green plankton in this icy pool are called sea ice algae.

Sea ice algae

? ? ?

Who ate the plankton?

A krill ate some plankton.

Antarctic krill

This tiny animal looks like a shrimp. It uses the fine hairs on its legs to trap plankton and bring them to its mouth.

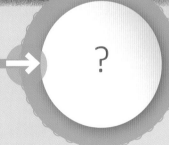

?

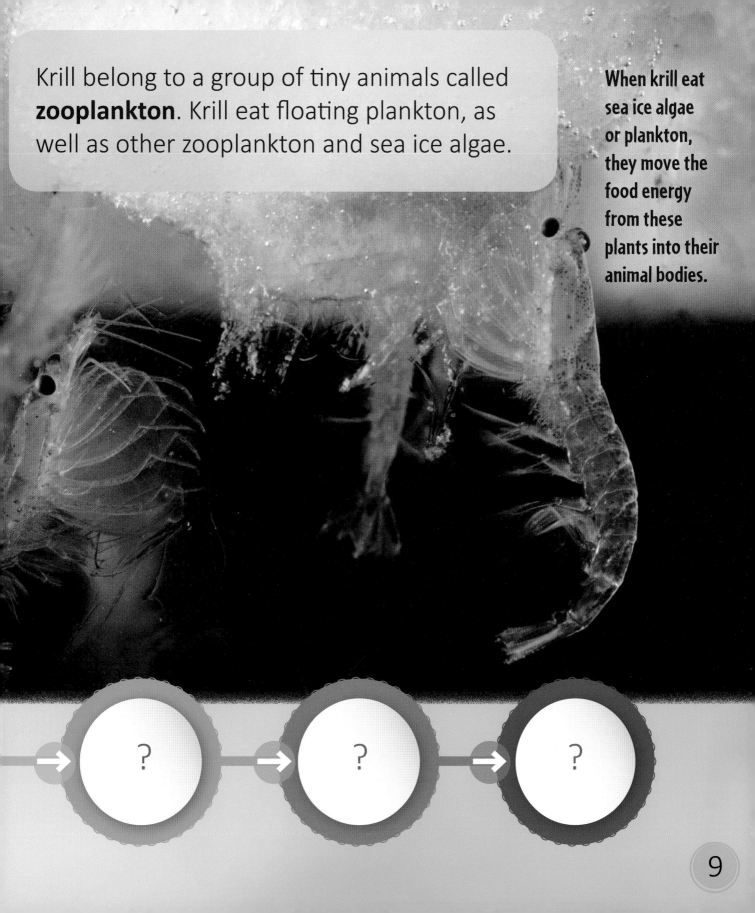

Krill belong to a group of tiny animals called **zooplankton**. Krill eat floating plankton, as well as other zooplankton and sea ice algae.

When krill eat sea ice algae or plankton, they move the food energy from these plants into their animal bodies.

Who ate the krill?

This time a small fish ate the krill.

Many Antarctic fish have special blood to stop them from freezing to death in the icy water.

Bald nototh̄en fish

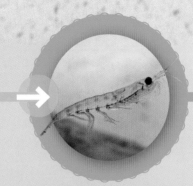

Most Antarctic animals eat krill. Fish, flying birds, seals, squid, penguins, and whales all eat krill.

These crabeater seals and birds are feasting on a swarm of krill.

↓ Humpback whale

Baleen plates

When a humpback whale takes in a mouthful of krill, it uses its tongue to press out the water. The krill get caught on the whale's **baleen plates**.

? ? ?

Who ate the fish?

This time a gentoo penguin ate the fish. It also eats krill and squid. The penguin moves its flippers to pull itself through the water.

Gentoo penguin

Bigger fish, whales, seals, penguins, and flying birds all eat small fish.

This weddell seal has come up to breathe through an ice hole.

Feeding penguin chicks

When an adult penguin has eaten many fish, it swims back to land where its chicks are waiting. One of the chicks chirps and the penguin brings up some fishy liquid from its stomach to feed it.

Soon it is time for the penguins to return to the ocean to hunt for more food. But a leopard seal is waiting in the water to catch a penguin to eat.

When the seal swims away, the penguins leap back into the water.

?   ?

Who ate the penguin?

A leopard seal ate the penguin.

The leopard seal hid under the water. When it saw the penguins in the ocean, it chased one onto some rocks. It then caught the penguin and ate it.

The seal doesn't like to eat the tough penguin skin. The skin floats down to the bottom of the ocean where other animals, such as starfish, eat it.

Who ate the leopard seal?

A leopard seal is a fierce **predator**. It eats many animals, including krill, squid, fish, seal pups, and penguins. Even as predators, leopard seals have to watch out.

Killer whales are bigger predators that like to eat seals. They also like to eat fish, squid, penguins, and even other whales. A killer whale is at the top of this Antarctic food chain.

Follow an ocean food chain

Energy from the Sun is made into food for plant plankton. Animals eat plankton, other animals, or a mix of both.

1

2

3

Can you remember the links in the
ocean food chain shown in this book?
The answers are at the bottom of
the page.

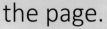

4

5

6

7

Who eats what?

Who eats what in a food chain depends on the food chain's location. There is no place on Earth like Antarctica.

The Antarctic has no trees, but millions of birds breed and nest here such as emperor penguins.

There are many threats to Antarctic food chains. Fishing boats in the Antarctic catch a lot of krill. This leaves less for penguins, seals, whales, fish, squid, and sea birds to eat.

Another threat is **global warming**, which is causing ice to melt. Seals need icebergs to rest on and to raise their pups. Fewer seals means less food for the animals that eat the seals.

Useful words

Antarctica The coldest continent on Earth, with the South Pole near its center. The land is covered in ice and surrounded by the Southern Ocean.

baleen plates Some whales have sheets of horn, called baleen, hanging from the roof of their mouth. The baleen is a bit like a comb.

energy The ability to move and do work. Food energy keeps a living thing alive and allows it to move, breathe, or work in some other way.

food chain The plants and animals linked together by what eats what

global warming The rise in temperature of Earth's atmosphere, which is the blanket of gases that surrounds our planet

microscope A device that uses lenses to make very small things appear larger

nutrient A substance that plants or animals need to live and grow

plant plankton A tiny plant that lives in water

predator An animal that hunts and eats other animals

sea ice algae Tiny plant plankton that live in and under sea ice

zooplankton A tiny animal that lives in water

Index